Carrot Creatures

Make Your Own

Iryna Stepanova

Sergiy Kabachenko

FIREFLY BOOKS

Contents

Introduction

Humans have been familiar with the carrot for more than four thousand years. Afghanistan and India are considered to be the origin of the wild carrot. There is historical evidence that the carrot was cultivated in Ancient Greece and Rome, but, in those days it was a rarity and was only served on major holidays. By the 14th to 16th centuries, the carrot in Europe was no longer a delicacy; French and German cookbooks contained many carrot dishes as, by that time, the common orange-red table carrot had already been widely cultivated in Holland. In Russia, the carrot became a widespread vegetable crop by the 17th century, and America, Australia and Canada joined the carrot revolution a short while later. In some countries, the carrot was even used at ritual ceremonies, and German legends state that dwarfs paid lavishly in gold for carrots.

A full complement of vitamins and minerals make this gift of nature a true source of health and longevity. Even better, cooking a carrot does not destroy its valuable qualities. On the contrary, new chemical compounds are formed, adding additional health-giving properties.

No fruit or vegetable equals the carrot in its high levels of beta-carotene, which is beneficial primarily for healthy skin, our immune system, and good eye health and vision.

Since ancient times, the healing properties of the carrot have been widely used—not only the root, but also the seeds and green tops. In this respect, Hippocrates considered it a leader among vegetables. The carrot has found wide application in the current treatment and prevention of various diseases. Owing to its low caloric content, it is also used in weight-loss regimes, and its unique chemical make-up makes it irreplaceable in cosmetic science and dermatology.

Mouse

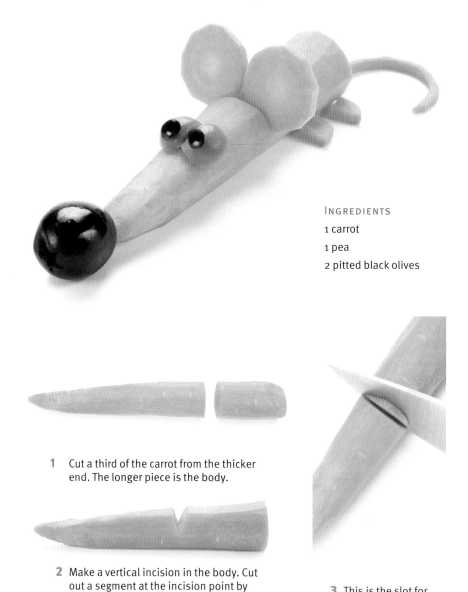

INGREDIENTS
1 carrot
1 pea
2 pitted black olives

1 Cut a third of the carrot from the thicker end. The longer piece is the body.

2 Make a vertical incision in the body. Cut out a segment at the incision point by angling the knife down toward the center of the incision.

3 This is the slot for the ears.

4 Cut four round slices from the shorter piece of carrot.

5 Put two slices into the slot. These are the ears.

6 Attach one olive to the pointy end of the body. This is the nose.

7 Cut the pea in half, without fully severing the two pieces.

8 Unfold the pea halves. These are the eyes.

9 Cut two small rounds from the other black olive. These are the pupils.

10 Place the pupils on the eyes.

11 Place the eyes on the muzzle.

12 Cut one of the round carrot slices into quarters. These are the legs.

13 Lay the legs against the body.

14 Using kitchen scissors, trim a thin strip off the remaining carrot slice. This is the tail.

15 Lay the tail against the mouse.

Seal

INGREDIENTS

2 carrots

1 pitted black olive

1 pitted green olive

1 Cut one carrot into three angled pieces.

2 The thicker piece is the body. Make two parallel incisions down the middle of the cut side and cut out the center strip to make a slot.

3 The middle angled piece is the neck. Make two parallel incisions in the wider end of the neck as in the body.

4 Cut the edge pieces off from each side of the incisions. These are the back flippers.

5 On the narrow end of the neck, make a slot for fastening the head.

6 The third angled piece of carrot is the head. Make two parallel incisions on the head as in step 4. Cut off the edge pieces.

7 Cut a thin strip lengthwise from the other carrot.

8 Cut the strip in half and round off the ends of each piece to make the front flippers.

9 Lay the front and back flippers against the body.

10 Attach the neck to the body. Then attach the head to the neck.

11 Cut the green olive in half without fully severing the two pieces.

12 Unfold the halves. These are the eyes.

13 Cut two small rounds from the black olive. These are the pupils. Place the pupils on the eyes.

14 Place the eyes on the head.

Dog

INGREDIENTS

2 carrots

2 pitted black olives

1 pitted green olive

2 corn kernels

4 peas

1 small round slice of
    red apple

chives

1 Cut a carrot into two pieces, one slightly longer than the other.

2 The shorter thicker piece is the lower part of the head. Cut off a slice lengthwise. This slice is the preform for the ears.

3 Place the head cut side down and cut out a triangular segment lengthwise from the rounded top.

4 Make a vertical incision close to one edge. Make a horizontal incision to remove the end pieces. This is the lower jaw, or muzzle.

5 Place two corn kernels on the cut out edge. These are the teeth. Cut a tongue out from the apple slice. Place the tongue between the teeth.

6 The remaining part of the carrot is the upper part of the head. Make an incision for the ears in the tip.

7 Cut the preform for the ears (step 2) in half lengthwise. Insert the ears into the incision. Place the upper part of the head onto the lower part.

8 Cut the black olive in half. One half is the nose. Lay the nose on the muzzle. Place a small piece of carrot on the muzzle as a support for the eyes.

9 Cut the green olive in half without fully severing the two pieces. Unfold the halves. These are the eyes.

10 Cut two small rounds from the black olive. These are the pupils.

11 Place the pupils on the eyes. Place the eyes on the head.

12 Lay the other whole carrot next to the head. This is the body. Make legs from the chives, and make hooves from the peas.

13 Use a slice of carrot for the tail.

Baby Bull

INGREDIENTS
1 carrot
1 corn kernel
1 pitted black olive
1 pitted black olive
2 pitted green olives

1 Cut a carrot into three parts.

2 The thicker end piece is the body. On one side, make a slot for the head.

3 On the other side, make four slots for the legs.

4 Cut a round slice from the middle piece of carrot and cut out a circle, leaving the horns.

5 Cut off a slice lengthwise from the middle piece of carrot. This is the preform for the ears. Cut off one more lengthwise strip.

6 Cut one strip into four parts. These are the legs.

7 Insert the legs into the slots on the body.

8 Set the body on the legs.

9 Cut the green olive in half lengthwise.

10 Cut each half in two.

11 Cut out triangular sections from each half to shape into hooves.

12 Place the hooves against the legs.

13 The remaining piece of carrot is the head. Make a slot at the top of the narrow end for the ears and horns.

14 Cut out an angled slot at the back of the narrow end of the head (refer to picture in step 16).

15 Cut a section from the wide end of the head as shown. This is the mouth.

16 Attach the head to the body.

17 Round the edges off the preform for the ears.

18 Insert the ears into the slot on the head.

19 Insert horns into the same slot.

20 Cut a slice lengthwise from the black olive.

21 Cut this in half. These are the lips.

22 Place the lips on the mouth as shown.

23 Make an incision in the corn kernel without fully severing the two pieces. Unfold the kernel halves. These are the eyes.

24 Cut two tiny rounds from the black olive. These are the pupils.

25 Place the pupils on the eyes.

26 Place the eyes on the head.

Lion

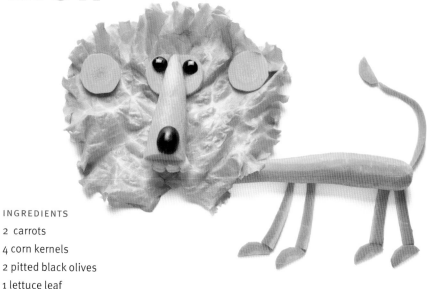

INGREDIENTS

2 carrots
4 corn kernels
2 pitted black olives
1 lettuce leaf

1 Cut a carrot in half and then cut three round slices from the narrow piece. The remaining part of the narrow half is the muzzle.

2 Make a slot in the wide end of the muzzle for the teeth.

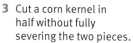

3 Cut a corn kernel in half without fully severing the two pieces.

4 Unfold the kernel halves. These are the teeth.

5 Make four such sets of teeth in total and insert them into the slot.

6 Place a lettuce leaf on a plate. This is the mane. Lay the muzzle on top.

7 Cut one round carrot slice in half. These are the eyes. Lay the eyes against the muzzle.

8 Cut two small rounds from an olive. These are the pupils.

9 Place the pupils on the eyes. Cut an olive in half lengthwise. Place one half on the muzzle. This is the nose.

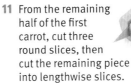

10 Use the other carrot for the body. Use two of the round carrot slices as ears. Please these on the mane.

11 From the remaining half of the first carrot, cut three round slices, then cut the remaining piece into lengthwise slices.

12 Cut two of the lengthwise slices into strips. These are the legs.

13 Cut two round slices in half. These are the paws.

14 Lay the paws against the legs. Cut another strip for the tail. Use half of a round slice for the tuft.

Tiger

INGREDIENTS

2 carrots
2 pitted black olives
1 pitted green olive
1 small slice of red apple

2 green peas
4 corn kernels
1 lettuce leaf

1 Cut a carrot into three pieces.

2 The thicker piece is the body. Make a slot in one end as shown for the neck.

3 Make a slot for the tail in the opposite end.

4 Turn over the body and make two slots for the legs.

5 Cut out legs as shown out of two round carrot slices.

6 Insert the legs into the slots.

7 The narrow piece of carrot is the neck. Cut out two pieces on the wider end as shown to create a plug to attach the neck to the body.

8 Attach the neck to the body.

9 Cut three thin round slices from a black olive. Make incisions around the inner edge. These are the stripes.

10 Lay the stripes on the body.

11 Cut a tail from a round carrot slice.

12 Insert the tail into the slot on the back end of the body. Use corn kernels for the paws.

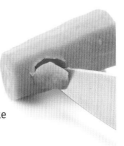

13 The middle part of the carrot is the head. Make a hole for the neck.

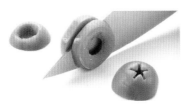

14 Make an incision for the mouth in the front part of the head, then make an incision for ears from the opposite edge. Insert a semicircular slice of the apple into the mouth. This is the tongue.

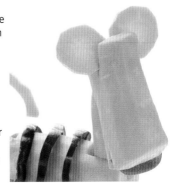

15 Use carrot rounds for ears and insert into the head. Fasten the head to the neck.

16 Cut the ends off the green olive. Cut the remaining middle part in half, without severing the two pieces.

17 Unfold the halves. These are the eyes. Place the eyes on the head. Insert the peas into the eyes and top each eye with a narrow slice of black olive for the pupils. Use an olive half for the nose.

Fir Tree

INGREDIENTS

1 carrot

green peas

1 lettuce leaf

1 Cut a round slice off the wide end of the carrot. Stand the carrot on the cut base. Using a vegetable peeler, make a thin, downward slice near the bottom of the carrot, almost to the base. Make more slices in the same way around the base of the carrot. This is the lower line of fir tree branches.

2 Make the next lines of branches in a chessboard pattern above the lower line.

3 Decorate the fir tree with green peas. Place it on the lettuce leaf.

Fox

INGREDIENTS

2 carrots
1 pitted black olive
1 pitted green olive
1 small slice of red
    apple peel

1 Choose a carrot with a very pointed end. This is the head. Make an incision for the mouth.

2 Make an incision for the ears on the opposite end of the head.

3 Cut the ends off the other carrot on an angle.

4 The end pieces are the body and tail.

5 Cut three oval slices from the middle piece of carrot.

6 Cut two of these in half lengthwise. These are the legs and ears.

7 Insert the ears into the incision in the head.

8 Cut the third oval slice in half. The two halves together make the mouth. Insert the mouth into the incision in the head.

9 Cut the green olive in half lengthwise, without completely severing the two pieces. Unfold the halves. These are the eyes. Cut out a small segment from each half.

10 Place the eyes on the head. Use half of the black olive for the nose.

11 Attach the body. Lay the legs against the body.

12 Attach the tail. Insert a thin slice of the red apple peel for the tongue.

Pirate

INGREDIENTS

3 carrots

4 pitted black olives

4 pitted green olives

1 sweet pea

lettuce leaf

1 Place the lettuce leaf on a plate. This is the beard. Place a carrot on top for the head.

2 Cut two round slices from another carrot. Lay these against the head. These are the ears.

3 Cut a round from a green olive. This is the mouth.

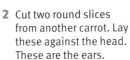

4 Cut a small piece on an angle off the wide end of a whole carrot.

5 Place this piece with the cut side down on the head. This is the nose.

6 Cut a green olive in half lengthwise, without fully severing the two pieces.

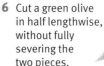

7 Unfold the halves. These are the eyes. Lay a pea on one eye and on top place a small round slice from a black olive. This is the pupil.

8 Cut a black olive in half. One half is the eye patch. Cover the second eye with the eye patch. Place the eyes on the head.

9 Attach a thin round and a whole black olive to the top of the head. This is the hat.

10 The remaining long angled piece of carrot is the body. Place the body under the lettuce below the head. Cut thin carrot strips for the arms.

11 Cut hands out of two round slices of carrot.

12 Place the hands against the arms. Use two green olives for the legs. Use a black olive cut in half for the boots.

Horse

INGREDIENTS

2 carrots
2 pitted black olives
2 corn kernels
2 stalks fresh dill

1 In the middle section of one carrot, make deep incisions in an alternating pattern on each side. On one side only, cut out segments from between the incisions.

2 This is the front of the neck.

3 Cut the end off the wide part of the carrot.

4 Stand the carrot cut side down.

5 Cut a small piece from the wide end of the other carrot. This is the body. Make a small incision in the rounded end for the tail.

6 Use a small dill stalk for the tail. Insert the tail into the body. Lay the body against the neck.

7 Insert corn kernels into the first incision on the neck. These are the eyes. Insert two of the carrot segments into the next incision. These are the ears.

8 Cut tiny rounds from a black olive. These are the pupils.

9 Place the pupils on the eyes.

10 Cut four carrot strips for the legs. Place these against the body.

11 Cut an olive in half lengthwise, then cut each half in two. These are the hooves.

12 Lay the hooves against the legs. Use the other dill stalk for the mane.

Hedgehog

INGREDIENTS

2 carrots

2 pitted black olives

1 pitted green olive

lettuce leaves

1 One whole carrot is the body. Carve the smaller end into a short point.

2 From the other carrot, cut two round slices in half. These are the legs.

3 Place the legs against the body.

4 Attach a black olive to the pointy end of the body for the nose.

5 Cut a green olive in half lengthwise, without fully severing the two pieces.

6 Unfold the halves and cut small segments out of each side. These are the eyes.

7 Cut similar-sized segments out of a black olive.

8 Insert these into the eyes. These are the pupils.

9 Place the eyes on the muzzle.

10 Place the salad leaves in a mound on top of the body. These are the quills.

Scorpion

INGREDIENTS

2 carrots
1 pitted black olive
1 pitted green olive
2 sweet peas

1 Lay one carrot flat and place a wooden chopstick on either side as knife guides. Make incisions starting a short way in from the wider end. Turn the carrot over, replace the chopsticks and make incisions between the ones made on the other side. See step 2 picture.

2 Cut out narrow segments from only one side of incisions. Insert these segments into the incisions on the opposite side. This will make the carrot bend. This is the tail.

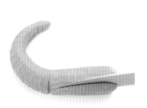

3 Cut a thin slice from one side of the carrot for stability.

4 Place the carrot cut side down. This is the scorpion.

5 Cut a thick round slice from the green olive, then cut the slice in half, without fully severing the two rings.

6 Unfold the rings and lay them on the scorpion. Place a pea in each ring.

7 Cut small rounds from the black olive.

8 Place the pupils on the peas. These are the eyes.

9 Cut ten quarter round slices from the other carrot.

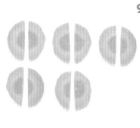

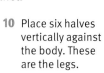

10 Place six halves vertically against the body. These are the legs.

11 Cut claws out of two halves.

12 Use the remaining halves, plus two more, for the forelegs, and attach the claws.

Frog

INGREDIENTS

1 carrot
1 pitted black olive
1 pitted green olive
2 corn kernels

1 Cut a carrot into three pieces. The narrow piece is the body.

2 Make an incision in the small end of the body for the forelegs, and another in the other end for the hindlegs.

3 Cut two round slices from the middle piece and two rounds from the third piece.

4 In each round, cut out two segments as shown. These will be the legs.

5 Cut fingers into the lower legs as shown.

6 Make two hindlegs and two forelegs.

7 Insert the hindlegs into the body.

8 Insert the forelegs.

9 Cut a narrow slice off each side of the middle piece of carrot.

10 Using an apple corer, make a vertical hole halfway into the middle piece. This is the head.

11 Make an incision with the knife and pop out the cut cylinder. This hole is for fastening the head.

12 Cut out a segment. This is the mouth.

13 Round off the head from all sides.

14 Place the head on the neck.

15 Insert corn kernels into the mouth for the teeth.

16 Cut the green olive in half for the eyes. Place on the head.

17 Cut a small round from the black olive.

18 Cut this in half. These are the pupils.

19 Place the pupils on the eyes.

Chameleon

INGREDIENTS

1 carrot

1 pitted black olive

2 pitted green olives

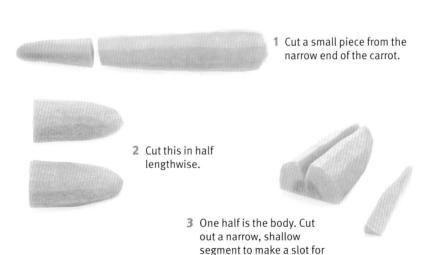

1 Cut a small piece from the narrow end of the carrot.

2 Cut this in half lengthwise.

3 One half is the body. Cut out a narrow, shallow segment to make a slot for the back crest.

4 Cut a thin slice from the remaining half.

5 Cut the crest out of it.

6 Insert the crest into the body (step 3).

7 Cut the remaining carrot piece in half. The wider piece is the preform for the head. Cut off one round slice.

8 Make a cut across one side of the preform. Cut out a segment holding the knife at an angle.

9 Cut a narrow segment from the other end of the preform. This is the mouth.

10 Cut out horns as shown. The eyes will be fastened onto these horns.

11 Stand the head on its base.

12 Cut the remaining middle piece of carrot in half lengthwise.

13 Cut a narrow slice from one half. Round off the edges.

14 Set the head on the rounded slice and put the body (step 6) on top.

15 Cut off one more narrow slice and cut a tail out of it.

16 Insert the tail into the slot in the body. Attach the green olives to the horns. These are the eyes.

17 Cut four half-rounds from the rest of the carrot.

18 Cut out the legs.

19 Place the legs against the body. Cut out a tongue from a narrow slice.

20 Cut two tiny rounds from a black olive. These are the pupils.

21 Lay the pupils on the eyes.

Turtle

INGREDIENTS

2 carrots

2 pitted black olives

2 sweet peas

1 Cut a small piece from the wide end of one carrot. This is the head. Using an apple corer, cut out a hole for an eye.

2 Remove the cut part with a knife. Make a second hole in the same way.

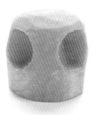

3 These are the eyes.

4 Cut out nostrils with the tip of a knife.

5 Cut a black olive in half.

6 Insert peas. These are the eyes. Cut two tiny rounds from the other black olive. These are the pupils.

7 Insert the eyes into the holes in the head.

8 Cut off a round carrot slice for the mouth. Cut a much smaller round slice and place on top of the mouth. This is the tongue.

9 Place the head on top of the tongue.

10 Use carrot rounds to make the shell.

11 Use more rounds to arrange the neck on top.

12 Lay out the remaining rounds row by row.

13 Cut out legs from four rounds.

14 Place the legs against the shell. Lay the head on the neck.

Crocodile

INGREDIENTS

2 carrots
1 pitted black olive
1 pitted green olive
2 corn kernels

1 Cut a narrow slice lengthwise from the middle of one carrot.

2 Cut the other carrot into thin rounds.

3 Arrange the carrot rounds on the slice, overlapping each other. This is the body.

4 Cut an oval slice from the remaining carrot. This is the head.

5 Lay the head on the body.

6 Cut an olive in half lengthwise, without fully severing the two pieces.

7 Unfold the halves and cut a narrow segment out of each half. These are the eyes.

8 Cut similarly-sized segments out of the black olive. These are the pupils.

9 Insert the pupils into the eyes. Lay the eyes on the head.

10 Place two corn kernels on the tip of the head for the teeth.

11 Lay half of a carrot round on top. This is the nose.

12 Cut out two legs from two carrot rounds.

13 Place the legs on the body.

Dragon

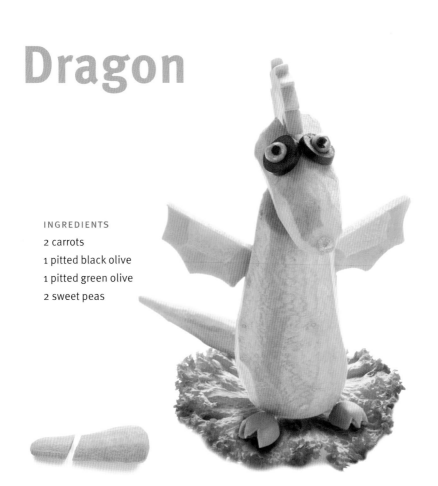

INGREDIENTS

2 carrots
1 pitted black olive
1 pitted green olive
2 sweet peas

1 Cut a carrot on an angle into two pieces, one slightly larger than the other. These are the preforms for the head and body.

2 The wider piece is the body. In the narrow end of the body, cut a rectangular slot on either side for the wings. Use an apple corer to make a hole for a tail in the lower middle part of the body with an apple corer.

3 Make an incision with the knife behind the hole in order to pop out the cut piece.

4 Cut off a round slice from the other carrot, then cut the slice in half.

5 Cut wings out of each half.

6 Insert the wings into the slots in the body.

7 Cut off the narrow end from the carrot. This is the tail. Insert the tail into the hole in the body.

8 Cut the green olive in half lengthwise. These are the paws. Cut out claws in each paw.

9 Lay the paws against the body.

10 Cut a thin slice from the preform for the head for stability.

11 Make a slot for the crest in the wide end of the head.

12 Place the head on the body.

13 Cut two rounds from the black olive for the eyes and two tiny rounds for the pupils. Insert a pea into each eye and lay the pupils on the eyes.

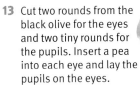

14 Cut a crest out of a carrot round.

15 Insert the crest into the slot in the head.

Bear

INGREDIENTS

2 carrots

2 pitted black olives

2 sweet peas

1 Cut a round slice from the wide end of one carrot. This is the body.

2 Cut out legs in the wide end of the body as shown. The remaining cut section is the preform for the head.

3 Lay the body on its side. Cut out a section for the head from the narrow end.

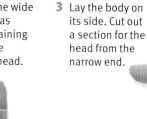

4 Stand the body on its legs and cut out paws.

5 Make a slot for the arms at the top of the body.

6 Cut a thin slice lengthwise from the other carrot.

7 Cut out arms from the slice.

8 Insert the arms into the slots in the body.

9 Make round slots in the preform about halfway deep for the eyes. Cut a hole all the way through for a nose.

10 Make a vertical incision in the top of the preform to pop out the cut parts.

11 Use two carrot rounds for the ears. Insert the ears into the incision.

12 Insert peas into the eye holes. Stick tiny rounds of black olive on the peas. These are the pupils.

13 Make an incision in one olive. Attach it to the carrot cylinder from the nose hole. This is the nose.

14 Insert the nose into the hole.

15 Place the head on the body. Insert a carrot round just under the head for the mouth.

Spider

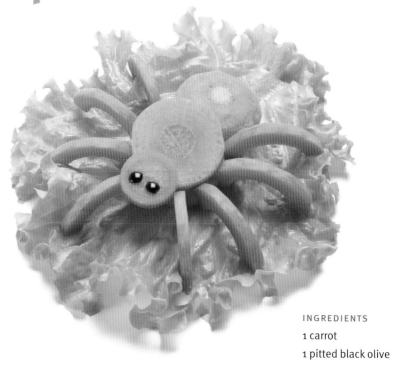

INGREDIENTS

1 carrot

1 pitted black olive

1 Cut a round slice from the wide end of the carrot. This is the hind part of the body.

2 Cut off five more rounds.

3 Use an apple corer to cut out a hole inside one round.

4 Cut this round in half. These are legs. Make four pairs of legs.

5 In another round, make slots around the edges for the legs.

6 Insert legs into the slots.

7 Rest the hind part of the body on the slotted round.

8 Cover with another whole round.

9 Cut tiny round slices from an olive. These are the eyes.

10 Place the eyes on a small carrot round. This is the head.

11 Lay the head on the body.

Boy

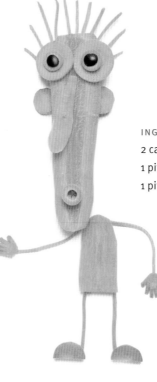

INGREDIENTS

2 carrots
1 pitted black olive
1 pitted green olive

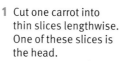

1 Cut one carrot into thin slices lengthwise. One of these slices is the head.

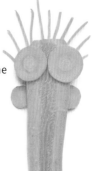

2 Cut another slice into strips. Arrange the strips on the head in the form of a hairstyle.

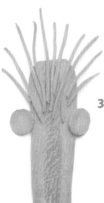

3 Cut two small round slices from the other carrot. Place the two rounds against the head. These are the ears.

4 Cover with one of the long slices. Cut two more larger rounds and place on the head for the eyes.

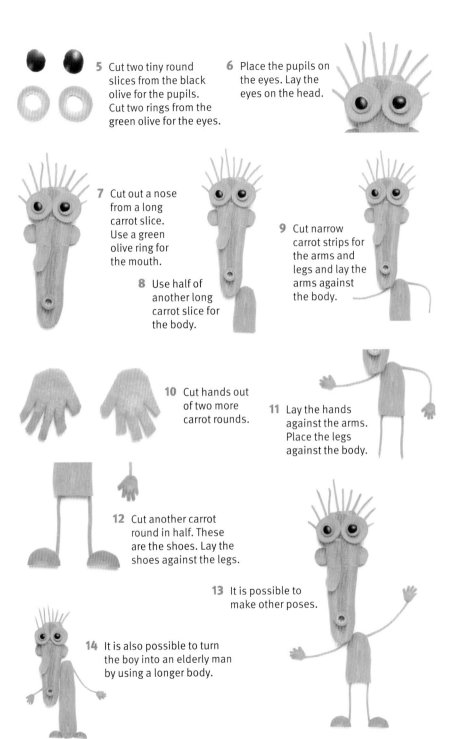

5 Cut two tiny round slices from the black olive for the pupils. Cut two rings from the green olive for the eyes.

6 Place the pupils on the eyes. Lay the eyes on the head.

7 Cut out a nose from a long carrot slice. Use a green olive ring for the mouth.

8 Use half of another long carrot slice for the body.

9 Cut narrow carrot strips for the arms and legs and lay the arms against the body.

10 Cut hands out of two more carrot rounds.

11 Lay the hands against the arms. Place the legs against the body.

12 Cut another carrot round in half. These are the shoes. Lay the shoes against the legs.

13 It is possible to make other poses.

14 It is also possible to turn the boy into an elderly man by using a longer body.

Sheep

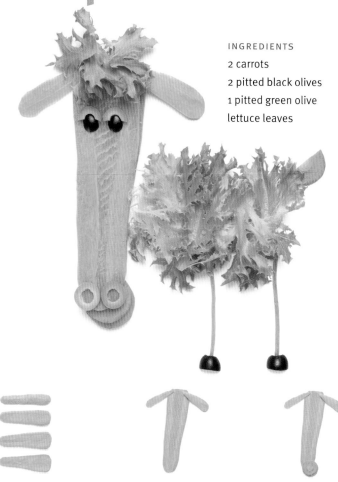

INGREDIENTS

2 carrots

2 pitted black olives

1 pitted green olive

lettuce leaves

1 Cut a carrot into thin slices lengthwise. One of these slices is the head.

2 Cut ears out of the smallest slice and lay the ears on the head.

3 Cut two small rounds from the other carrot and place on the tip of the head for the mouth. Cover the entire head with one more long slice.

4 Cut two round slices from a black olive. These are the eyes.

5 Place the eyes on the head.

6 Cut three rings from the green olive.

7 Cut one ring in half. These are the eyelids.

8 Lay the eyelids above the eyes. Place the other two rings on bottom of the head. This is the nose.

9 Arrange lettuce leaves for the body and place at top of head for the fringe.

10 Place two strips of carrot under the body for the legs.

11 Cut one half of the black olive in two. These are the hooves.

12 Attach the hooves to the legs.

13 Make a tail out of half of a carrot round.

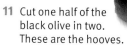

Ostrich

INGREDIENTS

1 carrot
1 pitted black olive
1 pitted green olive
lettuce leaves

1 Cut the carrot into thin slices lengthwise.

2 Arrange two slices as shown for the neck and the lower part of the head.

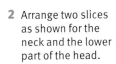

3 Stack another slice, slightly displaced, on top of the head.

4 Cut two tiny rounds from the black olive.

5 Place them on the head. These are the pupils.

6 Cut two rings from the green olive. Place them on top of the pupils. These are the eyes.

7 Use a small piece of lettuce for the crest.

8 Use more leaves to form the body.

9 Cut a carrot slice into strips.

10 Arrange the strips in the form of a tail.

11 Cut out upper thighs from another carrot slice.

12 Place the thighs against the body.

13 Use two carrot strips for the legs. Attach the legs to the thighs.

14 Cut a green olive ring in half. These are the feet. Lay them next to the legs.

Owl

INGREDIENTS
2 whole carrots
2 pitted black olives
1 pitted black olive

1 One of the carrots is the body. Make an incision at the larger end for the feet.

2 Cut a vertical flap about halfway up the body.

3 Cut a piece off the other carrot on angle. Cut three thin slices.

4 Cut two slices in half lengthwise.

5 Insert two halves in the slot.

6 Set the body upright.

7 Insert the other two halves in the flap.

8 The olive is the head. Make a slot in it for the beak.

9 Cut a beak from a carrot slice and insert in the head.

10 Cut two small thin carrot circles for eyes. Cut two tiny dots from a black olive for pupils. Place on the eyes.

11 Place the eyes on the head.

Bee

INGREDIENTS
1 carrot
1 pitted black olive
1 pitted green olive
lettuce leaves

1 Cut one carrot into thin slices lengthwise.

2 Cut two of the slices into two unequal parts. The two larger pieces are part of the body. One of the smaller pieces is the head.

3 Cut the second smaller piece into strips.

4 On one of the body pieces, arrange three strips for the legs.

5 From one of the long
slices, cut out two
wings and place on
the body.

6 Cover with the
second body piece.

7 Cut the end off the
green olive for the
mouth. Then cut two
rings for the eyes.

8 Place the eyes
on the head.

9 Cut two tiny rounds
from a black olive.
These are the pupils.

10 Place the pupils on
the eyes.

11 Cut a narrow carrot
strip for the antenna.

12 Place the mouth on
the head.

13 Place the head
on the body.

14 Arrange the strips
on the body for
the stripes.

Girl

INGREDIENTS

3 carrots
1 pitted black olive
2 pitted green olives
2 corn kernels
lettuce leaves

1 Lay a lettuce leaf. It is the hair

2 Slice a carrot in half lengthwise. Place one half on the lettuce leaf. This is the head.

3 Cut a green olive in half lengthwise without fully severing it. Unfold the halves.

4 Cut out small horizontal segments. These are the eyes.

5 Put the eyes on the head.

6 Cut obliquely a small slice from the whole carrot. Lay it with the cut upwards. It is a nose.

7 Cut the other green olive in half, for the mouth. The corn kernels are the teeth.

8 Insert the teeth in the mouth.

9 Lay the mouth under the nose.

10 Cut thin bars out of the third carrot.

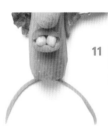 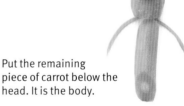

11 Lay two of them below the head. These are arms.

12 Put the remaining piece of carrot below the head. It is the body.

13 Lay the legs below the body. Cut the other black olive in half crosswise without fully severing it. Unfold the halves and lay on the body.

14 Use a lettuce leaf for a skirt.

Centipede

INGREDIENTS

1 carrot
1 pitted black olive
1 pitted green olive
1 sweet pea
corn kernels
chives

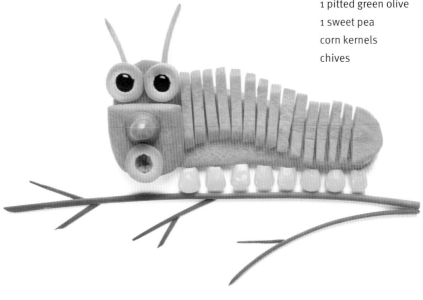

1 Cut a carrot into thin slices lengthwise.

2 Cut a piece off the end of one of the slices. This is the muzzle. Cut the remaining slice into strips as shown.

3 Arrange the strips in a wave form on top of another slice. This is the body.

4 Cut off two thin strips. These are the antennae.

5 Place a small round carrot slice on top. This is the head.

6 Place the muzzle on the head.

7 Cut two tiny rounds from the black olive. These are the pupils.

8 Lay the pupils on the head.

9 Cut the ends off the green olive. Cut the remaining middle part into two rings. These are the eyes.

10 Lay the eyes over the pupils and place the cut olive ends on the muzzle as shown for the mouth and nose.

11 Place the pea on the nose.

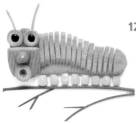 

12 Use the corn kernels for the legs. Arrange the chives underneath as a leaf.

13 It is a possible to arrange the centipede on a lettuce leaf.

Fish

INGREDIENTS

2 carrots
1 pitted black olive
1 pitted green olive
corn kernels
green onion stalks
lettuce leaves

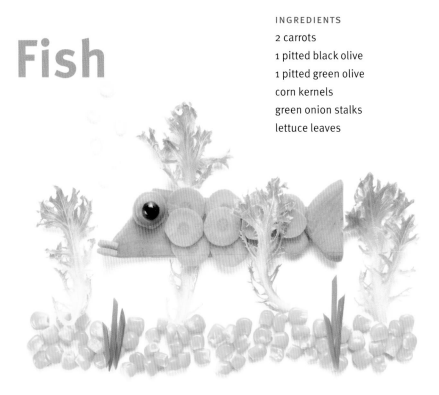

1 Cut a thin, flat slice lengthwise from one carrot. Cut an angled piece from the wide part of the slice. This is the tail. The remaining part is the body and the pointed end is the head.

2 Cut a thin carrot into rounds.

3 Cut the smallest round in half.

60

4 Cut slots in each half that are the same width as the end of the head. These are the lips.

5 Attach the lips to the head.

6 Place the tail on the opposite end.

7 Use the carrot rounds to make two rows of scales.

8 Place one more centered line of scales on top.

9 Place one more round on the head. This is the base for the eye.

10 Cut the edge off a green olive half.

11 Cut a tiny round from the black olive. This is the pupil.

12 Place the pupil on the cut edge of the green olive half. This is the eye.

13 Place the eye on its base. Make a sea bed of corn, add lettuce leaves and green onion stalks for seaweed. Cut several thin slices from the white part of the onion, separate them into rings and arrange above the fish for bubbles.

Poodle

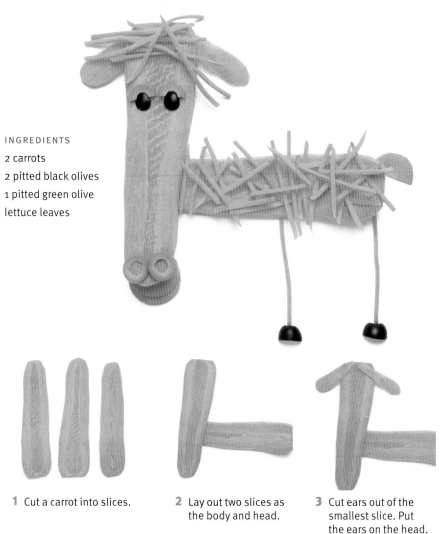

INGREDIENTS

2 carrots
2 pitted black olives
1 pitted green olive
lettuce leaves

1 Cut a carrot into slices.

2 Lay out two slices as the body and head.

3 Cut ears out of the smallest slice. Put the ears on the head.

4 Place two carrot rounds at the end of the head, as shown. Cover the head with another slice.

5 Cut two round slices from an olive. These are eyes. Lay the eyes on the head.

6 Cut three rings from a green olive.

7 Cut one ring in half. These are eyelids. Lay the eyelids above the eyes.

8 Lay two whole rings on the muzzle as the nose.

9 Cut a carrot into bars. Lay the bars in the form of a body and a fringe.

10 Lay two carrot bars under the body as legs.

11 Cut the black olive half into two pieces. These are hoofs. Lay them by the legs.

12 Use half of a carrot circle for the tail.

Cat

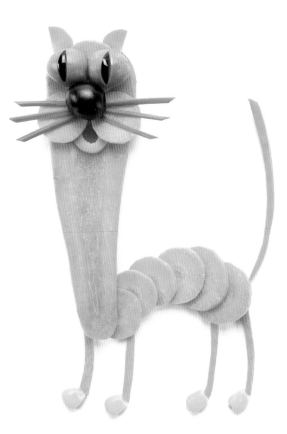

INGREDIENTS

2 carrots
2 pitted black olives
1 pitted green olive
4 corn kernels
chives

1 Cut one thin flat slice from a carrot. This is the neck and head.

2 Cut the other whole carrot into rounds.

3 Cut the smallest round in half. These are the ears.

4 Put the ears at the top of the head. Put a carrot round on top. Put a green olive below the round. This is the mouth.

5 Place two rounds over the mouth. These are the cheeks.

6 Cut two narrow segments out of a black olive. These are the pupils.

7 Cut the green olive in half lengthwise. Cut out segments out of each half in the same size as the black olive segments. These are the eyes.

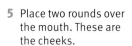

8 Insert the pupils into the eyes. Place the eyes on the round. Use two rounds to make the cheeks. This is the head.

9 Cut a black olive in half. One half is the nose.

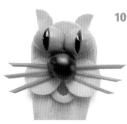

10 Place the nose over the cheeks. Cut chives into six parts. These are the whiskers. Place them below the nose.

11 Arrange the carrot rounds in the form of a body.

12 Cut thin carrot strips for the legs and tail. Attach these to the body.

13 Use the corn kernels for the paws.

African Landscape

INGREDIENTS

2 carrots
1 pitted black olive
1 pitted green olive
lettuce leaf
corn kernels

1 Cut a thin flat slice from one carrot lengthwise. This is the tree trunk.

2 Cut two narrow carrot strips. Place them against the trunk. These are branches.

3 Arrange carrot rounds around the top of the trunk for the treetop.

4 Attach more rounds to the branches. Decorate the base of the trunk with a lettuce leaf.

5 Cut one small and one large carrot round in half.

6 Place the two small halves under one of the big halves. These are the ears and head.

7 Cut a thin strip of carrot in half to make the horns. Lay the horns between the ears.

8 Cut a round slice from the black olive.

9 Cut the slice in half. These are the eyes.

10 Lay the eyes on the head.

11 Use a long thin carrot strip for the neck. Use a carrot round for the body.

12 Use more carrot strips for the legs and tail.

13 Cut the green olive in half, then cut one half in two. These are the hooves. Arrange the corn kernels as sand.

Roses

INGREDIENTS

1 large carrot
1 lettuce leaf

1 Cut the carrot into thin
round slices.

2 Simmer the rounds in
water for 5 minutes,
then take them out and
let them cool.

3 Lay out the rounds
in a row overlapping
each other.

4 Tightly roll up the row into a tube.

5 Carefully cut the tube in half to create two roses.

6 Set the roses with the cut side down.

7 To make a bud, cut three of the cooked carrot rounds in half.

8 Lay out the halves in a row, overlapping each other.

9 Roll them up tightly into a tube.

10 Cut out a leaf with a toothed edge from a raw carrot round.

11 Cut out a vertical vein in the center of the leaf.

12 Cut out side veins from the central line.

Rabbit

INGREDIENTS

1 large carrot
1 pitted black olive
1 pitted green olive
2 corn kernels

1 Cut out a segment from the wide end of the carrot.

2 Make vertical incisions in the center of the cut area. Cut out a slice of carrot. These are legs.

3 Make a hole for a nose on the narrow side of the carrot. Make a slot for the ears at the top.

4 Make two narrow, parallel slots for arms, one on each side.

5 Cut ears out of a large, round carrot slice.

6 Insert the ears into the slot.

7 Make a horizontal incision on one side of the green olive. Cut the corn kernels in half lengthwise, without fully severing the halves. Insert half of each corn kernel into the incision on the olive, allowing the other half to hang over the edge. This is the nose with teeth.

8 Insert the nose into the hole.

9 Cut one more big carrot round in half. Make a hole in one half using an apple corer.

10 These are the cheeks. Hang them on the nose.

11 Cut out the base for the eyes from the second carrot half as shown.

12 Cut small rounds from the olive. These are the eyes. Stick them onto the eye base. Insert the eyes above the nose.

13 Cut arms out of two more carrot rounds.

14 Insert the arms into the slots.

Wolf

INGREDIENTS

1 big carrot

1 small carrot

2 pitted black olives

1 Cut out a segment from the wide end of a carrot.

2 Make two vertical incisions as shown.

3 Cut out the piece between the two incisions. These are the legs. Cut off the top section of the legs. The remaining part is the body.

4 Stand the body on its legs and make two slots at the top for the arms.

5 Cut out a segment from the top for stabilizing the head.

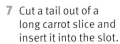

6 Make a slot from behind for fastening a tail.

7 Cut a tail out of a long carrot slice and insert it into the slot.

8 Make arms out of carrot strips and insert into side slots.

9 Cut a piece from the other carrot near the wider end.

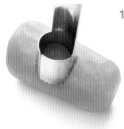

10 Round off the sides in order to make an oval-shaped head. Cut a groove in the center for fastening the muzzle.

11 Make two incisions at the top for the ears.

12 Cut a carrot round in half. These are the ears. Insert the ears into the incisions.

13 Cut off the narrow end of the carrot. This is the muzzle. Cut out a pin on the wider side for fastening the nose.

14 Use a black olive for the nose and attach to the muzzle (step 10). Insert the muzzle into the hole. Place the head on the body.

15 Use two carrot rounds for the eyes, and two small rounds of black olive for the pupils.

Aster

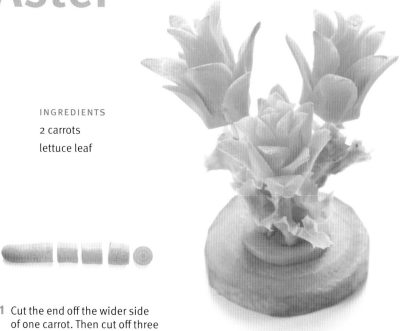

1 Cut the end off the wider side of one carrot. Then cut off three thick slices. These are preforms for the flowers.

2 Stand one preform on the cut side and cut off a slice, holding the knife at an outward angle.

3 Cut off slices in the same way from all four sides. It should look like a pyramid with four sides and a flat top.

4 Make a hollow in one corner. This is the base for a petal.

5 Cut off a thin petal, not reaching the bottom of the preform.

6 Cut more petals around the lower row.

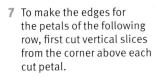

7 To make the edges for the petals of the following row, first cut vertical slices from the corner above each cut petal.

8 Now the corners are placed between the petals of the first row.

9 Cut the second row of petals off the corners.

10 Repeat step 7 above to make the next row of petals.

11 Cut the third row of petals.

12 Cut off the top from the middle of the flower.

13 Cut apart the middle into four parts.

14 Cut two more flowers out of the two remaining preforms.

15 Decorate with lettuce leaves. Or, insert toothpicks into the base of each flower. Insert the flowers into a large slice of carrot, and decorate with lettuce leaves.

Clown

INGREDIENTS

1 large carrot
1 small carrot
2 pitted black olives
2 pitted green olives
1 lettuce leaf
1 corn kernel

1 Cut the large carrot into two pieces, one longer than the other. The wider piece is the body. The narrow piece is the head.

2 Make slots for the arms in the upper part of the body.

3 Cut a thin slice lengthwise from the other carrot. Cut it in half again lengthwise.

4 Cut out an arm (with a hand) from each half.

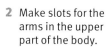

5 Make a square incision in a carrot round. This is the cuff.

6 Place the cuff on the arm.

7 Insert the arms into the slots in the body. Attach three rings from a green olive for the buttons.

8 Cut a carrot round in half and round off one edge on each half. These are the soles of the boots.

9 Cut a black olive into quarters. Two quarters are the toes of the boots.

10 Place the toes on the boots.

11 Cut short carrot strips. Place these on the boots for the laces.

12 Lay the boots against the clown.

13 Place a large carrot round on the body. This is the ruffle. Place a small, slightly thicker round on top for the neck.

14 Make a triangular incision in the near the top center of the head for fastening the nose. Make an incision at the top of the head for fastening the wig.

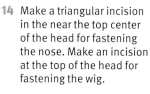

15 Insert a lettuce leaf into the incision. This is the wig.

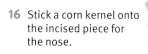

16 Stick a corn kernel onto the incised piece for the nose.

17 Cut two round slices from the sides of a black olive, one of which is the mouth. Cut the other slice in half. These are the eyes.

18 Place the mouth and eyes on the face.

19 Use green olive rings for the glasses. Place over the eyes. Place the head on the neck.

Grandpa

INGREDIENTS

1 large carrot
1 small carrot
1 pitted black olive
1 pitted green olive
1 lettuce leaf
1 corn kernel

1 Cut a carrot into three parts. The wider end piece is the body. The narrow end piece is the head.

2 Make two incisions in the upper part of the body.

3 Cut out the piece between the incisions to make legs.

4 Stand the body on the legs and cut out a triangular segment in the upper part for attaching head.

5 Make slots on each side of the top for fastening the arms.

6 Cut a carrot round in half. These are the preforms for arms.

7 First, cut out the fingers.

8 Then cut out the arms.

9 Round off the shoulder.

10 Cut the remaining middle piece of carrot in half lengthwise.

11 Lay both with the cut side down and cut out boots as shown.

12 Round off the toes of the boots

13 Insert the arms into the top slots and insert the legs into the boots.

14 Cut out a chin from the preform for the head.

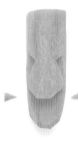

15 Cut out triangular hollows for eyes.

16 Round off the nose.

17 Cut out a triangular section to make the mouth.

18 Cut a hole in the middle of a carrot round. This is the hat brim.

19 Place the brim on the head.

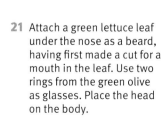

20 Use two small rounds of black olive for the eyes.

21 Attach a green lettuce leaf under the nose as a beard, having first made a cut for a mouth in the leaf. Use two rings from the green olive as glasses. Place the head on the body.

Butterflies

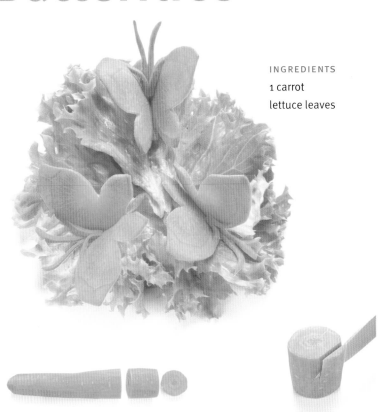

INGREDIENTS

1 carrot

lettuce leaves

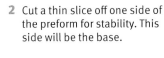

1 Cut the end off the thick end of the carrot, then another small piece. This piece is the preform for the butterfly.

2 Cut a thin slice off one side of the preform for stability. This side will be the base.

3 Cut one more such slice from the preform next to the first one. This is the back surface of the wings.

4 Place the carrot on its base. Cut a big slice from one side. This is the external surface of the wings.

5 Cut out a small segment. This is an internal part between the wings.

6 Set the preform on its base and cut off the corners, smoothing out the lines of the wings.

7 Cut out a small segment between the base and the smaller back wing.

8 Put the preform back on its base and cut off a thin slice parallel to the shape of the wing, without cutting all the way to the base of the preform.

9 Cut the second wing in the same way.

10 Lay the butterfly on its base. Cut out short antennae.

11 Make a slot under the antennae as shown.

12 Carefully move the wings slightly apart.

13 Cut a piece of short antennae and insert them between the wings.

14 Arrange the butterflies on a lettuce leaf.

Sunflower

INGREDIENTS

1 carrot

lettuce leaf

3 stalks green onion

1 Cut three thick round slices from the carrot. These are preforms for the flowers.

2 Core one round halfway through.

3 Cut away the upper part of the preform around the corer using a knife.

4 This will leave a small cylinder in the center of the preform.

5 Round off the edges of the preform with a knife.

6 Cut out petals around the preform as shown.

7 Score the center of the cylinder.

8 Make two more grooves.

9 Make more grooves at a right angle to create a net pattern.

10 Cut a leaf out of a carrot slice.

11 Smooth out leaf edges.

12 Cut out a narrow groove in the center of the leaf.

13 Cut out veins.

14 Cut out teeth around the edge.

15 Place green onion stalks against the sunflower. Lay the carrot leaves against the stalks. Make a flowerbed from carrot slices and lettuce leaves.

Tulips

INGREDIENTS

1 carrot
lettuce leaf
green onion stalks

1 Cut three preforms from the carrot as shown.

2 Round off the edges.

3 Round off the bottom.

4 Round off all three preforms on one side.

5 Cut a petal on one side of a preform as shown.

86

6 Make an incision behind the petal as close as possible without severing the petal from the base.

7 Cut three more petals in the same way.

8 Make a small incision at the bottom of the petals with a narrow knife.

9 Carefully separate the petals and cut out the preform.

10 Make the preform cylindrical.

11 Make petals in this preform following steps 5 to 9.

12 Insert smaller petals into the middle of the larger petals. This is the tulip.

13 Make three more tulips.

14 Attach a green onion stalk to each tulip.

15 Make a flowerbed from a lettuce leaf.

Train

INGREDIENTS

3 carrots

2 pitted green olives

1 Cut one carrot into two unequal parts as shown.

2 Stand the short piece cut side down and cut vertical slices from all sides to make it rectangular. This is the cab.

3 Cut a platform for the roof from the top.

4 Cut out a window.

5 Cut six preforms for wheels from the remaining part of the carrot.

6 Insert an apple corer halfway into a preform. With a knife, cut away the upper part of the preform around the corer.

7 Do this with the other five wheels

8 Trim the sides to make a square form, as shown. This is the undercarriage, or platform.

9 Using the corer, make three holes all the way through the side of the platform. Cut off the tip at an angle.

10 Insert the wheels into the holes.

11 Attach an olive ring to each wheel. Place the cabin on the platform.

12 Cut a piece from the rounded end of carrot. Cut a thin side slice lengthwise. This is the boiler.

13 Set it on the platform. Make a hole in the top for a pipe.

14 Using the side slices, cut a roof for the cab and a grille for the front of the platform.

15 Use one of the cylindrical cut-outs from the platform as a smokestack. Insert it into the boiler hole. You can also make extra cars, as shown.

Chrysanthemum

INGREDIENTS
1 carrot
lettuce leaf

1 Cut a slice off the thick end of the carrot.

2 Cut a short piece from the wide end of the carrot. This is the preform.

3 Cut a thin layer from the circumpherence of the carrot as shown, making it as long as possible without breaking.

4 Soften the resulting ribbon for half an hour in extremely salty water.

5 Make incisions along the whole length of the ribbon, but do not cut completely.

6 Fold the ribbon in half lengthwise.

7 Carefully roll it up as shown.

8 This is the chrysanthemum.

9 Cut a leaf out of a long slice of carrot.

10 Cut out teeth around the edge of the leaf. Make several such leaves.

11 Arrange thin carrot strips as small stalks.

12 Attach the leaves.

13 Attach the chrysanthemum. Decorate the base with the lettuce leaf.

Truck

INGREDIENTS

2 carrots

2 pitted green olives

1 pitted black olive

1 Cut a carrot into three pieces.

2 Cut four thick rounds from the narrow piece. These are the preforms for the wheels.

3 Insert an apple corer halfway into each preform. Cut away the upper part of each preform with a knife.

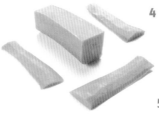

4 Cut the sides off of the middle piece of carrot to make it rectangular. This is the tractor unit, or frame.

5 With the apple corer, make two holes all the way through the side of the frame. Insert the wheels into the holes.

6 Cut four small round slices from a black olive. These are the hubcaps. Insert them in the wheels.

7 Cut a lengthwise, slightly thicker slice from the remaining piece of carrot. Cut out sections on each side as shown so that one end is the same width as the frame.

8 Cut out pins for fastening headlights into the wider part of the slice.

9 Cut out two green olive rings for the lights and attach to the pins. Place the slice on the frame.

10 Cut a piece from the wide end of a whole carrot. Trim all sides to make it rectangular. This is the cab.

11 Cut out side windows.

12 Cut out a windshield.

13 Set the cab on the frame.

14 Cut a piece from the remaining carrot. Round it the form of a tank.

15 Set the tank on the frame.

Flower

1 carrot

lettuce leaves

1 Using a vegetable peeler, cut the carrot into thin strips. Let the strips sit until they have faded a bit.

2 Cut the thick end off the carrot.

3 Stand this piece cut side down. Make a vertical incision.

4 Cut out a thin slice of the carrot above the incision.

5 Make three more such incisions. This is the base of the flower.

6 Choose the four biggest carrot strips. If needed, trim so that they are equal in size.

7 Fold up a strip in the form of an eyelet, as shown. This is a petal.

8 Insert the folded ends of the petal into one of the incisions in the base.

9 Make three more petals and insert them into the other sides of the base.

10 Round the edges of the narrowest strip and roll it up.

11 Place it on the center of the base.

12 Cut two more narrow strips in half.

13 Fold each strip in the form of an eyelet.

14 Insert the folded ends above the bigger petals, only facing in reverse.

15 Cut thin strips from the remaining piece of carrot to decorate the flower.

A FIREFLY BOOK

Published by Firefly Books Ltd. 2016

First printing

PUBLISHER CATALOGING-IN-PUBLICATION DATA (U.S.)
Names: Stepanova, Iryna, author. | Kabachenko, Sergiy, author.
Title: Carrot creatures : make your own / Iryna Stepanova, Sergiy Kabachenko.
Description: Richmond Hill, Ontario, Canada : Firefly Books, 2016. | Series: Make Your Own | Summary: Food presentation skills for cooks, chefs, and parents are provided with step by step instructions and photographs of each step.
Identifiers: ISBN 978-1-77085-854-1 (hardcover)
Subjects: LCSH: Cooking (Carrots). | Food presentation. | Garnishes (Cooking)
Classification: LCC TX740.5S747 | DDC 641.819 – dc23

LIBRARY AND ARCHIVES CANADA CATALOGUING IN PUBLICATION
Stepanova, Iryna, author
Carrot creatures : make your own / Iryna Stepanova and Sergiy Kabachenko.
(Make your own ; 2)
ISBN 978-1-77085-854-1 (hardback)
1. Food craft. 2. Food presentation. 3. Cooking (Garnishes).
4. Cooking (Carrots). I. Kabachenko, Sergiy, author II. Title.
TX740.5.S74 2016   745.5   C2016-903715-0

Published in the United States by
Firefly Books (U.S.) Inc.
P.O. Box 1338, Ellicott Station
Buffalo, New York 14205

Published in Canada by
Firefly Books Ltd.
50 Staples Avenue, Unit 1
Richmond Hill, Ontario L4B 0A7

Cover and interior design: Peter Ross / Counterpunch Inc.

Printed in China

The publisher gratefully acknowledges the financial support for our publishing program by the Government of Canada through the Canada Book Fund as administered by the Department of Canadian Heritage.